In the Sky

The Planets

by Carol Ryback

Reading consultant: Susan Nations, M.Ed., author/literacy coach/
consultant in literacy development

Please visit our web site at: www.earlyliteracy.cc
For a free color catalog describing Weekly Reader® Early Learning Library's
list of high-quality books, call 1-877-445-5824 (USA) or 1-800-387-3178 (Canada).
Weekly Reader® Early Learning Library's fax: (414) 336-0164.

Library of Congress Cataloging-in-Publication Data

Ryback, Carol.
    The planets / by Carol Ryback.
      p. cm. — (In the sky)
    Includes bibliographical references and index.
    ISBN 0-8368-6344-5 (lib. bdg.)
    ISBN 0-8368-6349-6 (softcover)
    1. Planets—Juvenile literature. I. Title.
  QB602.R93 2006
  523.4—dc22   2005026535

This edition first published in 2006 by
Weekly Reader® Early Learning Library
A Member of the WRC Media Family of Companies
330 West Olive Street, Suite 100
Milwaukee, WI 53212 USA

Copyright © 2006 by Weekly Reader® Early Learning Library

Series editor: Dorothy L. Gibbs
Editor: Barbara Kiely Miller
Art direction, cover and layout design: Tammy West
Photo research: Diane Laska-Swanke

Photo credits: Cover, title, pp. 5, 9, 10, 11, 13, 16 (upper and lower right), 20 NASA; p. 6
© North Wind Picture Archives; p. 7 (left) © Corel; pp. 7 (right), 21 NASA Goddard Space Flight
Center; p. 12 U.S. Geological Survey; p. 13 NASA/JPL/Cornell; p. 15 NASA/JPL; p. 16 (lower left)
JPL; pp. 17, 19 NSSDC and the Team Leader, Dr. Bradford A. Smith

Printed in the United States of America

1 2 3 4 5 6 7 8 9 10 09 08 07 06

Table of Contents

CHAPTER 1 A Parade of Planets 4

CHAPTER 2 The Rocky Planets 8

CHAPTER 3 Great Balls of Gas 14

CHAPTER 4 Far Out in Space 18

Glossary 22

For More Information .23

Index 24

On the cover and title page: The planets are shown in the order in which they circle the Sun. Earth is the the third planet from the Sun.

A Parade of Planets

Not all of the bright spots in the night sky
are stars. Some of those spots are planets.
A planet does not make its own light. Light from
the same Sun that shines on Earth shines on a
parade of planets that we can see from Earth.

Earth's place in space is called the **solar system**. Earth's solar system includes the Sun and its planets. The Sun is the center of the solar system. All the planets, including Earth, circle around, or **orbit**, the Sun. Each planet follows a different orbit around the Sun.

The planets are different sizes, but not one comes close to being as big as the Sun.

SUN

NEPTUNE

SATURN

MARS

VENUS

EARTH

JUPITER

URANUS

PLUTO

MERCURY

The names of the planets, in order, starting closest to the Sun, are Mercury, Venus, Earth, Mars, Jupiter, Saturn, Uranus, Neptune, and Pluto. To remember the names of the planets, just think of this sentence: **M**y **V**ery **E**ducated **M**other **J**ust **S**erved **U**s **N**ine **P**izzas. The first letter of each word stands for the name of a planet.

Many planets are named after Roman gods.
This picture shows a statue of the Roman god Jupiter.

The planets are different sizes and colors. No two planets are alike. Some planets are very hot. Others are very cold. Some are made of rocks. Others are mostly gases. All of the planets spin. Some spin fast. Some spin slow. Four planets have rings. Seven planets have at least one moon.

Earth (*left*) and Mars (*right*) orbit the Sun next to each other in space, but the planets look very different up close.

CHAPTER

The Rocky Planets

Mercury is the planet closest to the Sun. This planet does not have any air or water. It is a tiny, dry, and rocky planet. Nothing lives on Mercury. One year on a planet is the number of days it takes that planet to circle the Sun. Mercury circles the Sun faster than any other planet. One year on Mercury lasts only eighty-eight Earth days.

Venus is the second planet from the Sun. It is about the same size as Earth, but it is not at all like Earth. Venus does not have any water, and people would not be able to breathe the air on Venus. Volcanoes on Venus give off poisonous gases. The gases form poisonous clouds over the planet. The clouds hold in the Sun's heat, which makes Venus too hot for animals or plants to live there.

Venus is covered with volcanoes that pour out poisonous gases and hot, liquid rocks. Venus is unsafe for any kind of life.

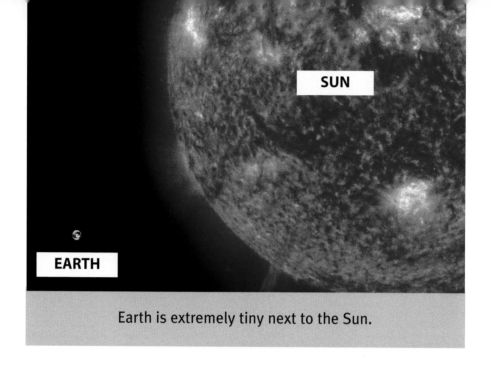

SUN

EARTH

Earth is extremely tiny next to the Sun.

Our planet, Earth, is the third rocky planet from the Sun. Earth is the only planet in our solar system that has air and water — and life! Although it seems like a big planet, Earth is small compared to the Sun. If the Sun were the size of a basketball, Earth would be about half the size of the eraser on your pencil. Think how small your house would be!

Earth spins completely around once every twenty-four hours. We call that amount of time one day. Earth is about 93 million miles (150 million kilometers) from the Sun. Earth orbits the Sun once every 365 days. We call that time one year. How many times in your life have you orbited the Sun?

Earth has one Moon. This is the first picture ever taken that shows Earth and the Moon at the same time.

Olympus Mons on Mars is the largest volcano on any planet in the solar system.

Mars is the fourth planet from the Sun. Red rocks and dust cover Mars, so people also call it the "Red Planet." Mars is about half the size of Earth. It has the highest mountains and the deepest canyons of any planet in the solar system.

People have not traveled to Mars, but spacecraft have landed there. The spacecraft carried robot vehicles called **rovers**. Some of the rovers explored the surface of Mars. They took many pictures and ran scientific tests.

The *Opportunity* rover took a picture of one of the many craters on the Red Planet.

CHAPTER

Great Balls of Gas

The largest planets in the solar system are made mostly of gases. These planets are called gas giants. Jupiter is the biggest gas giant. Strong winds on Jupiter move its gases around the planet. One area, called the Great Red Spot, is a giant storm of twisting gases.

Jupiter is so big that it weighs more than all the other eight planets put together! Jupiter is also a fast-spinning planet. It spins much faster than Earth. One day on Jupiter lasts only about ten hours on Earth.

In 1977, astronomers discovered rings around Jupiter. The smaller bodies shown here are three of Jupiter's many moons.

RINGS

MOONS

Saturn is often called the "ringed planet." Its rings are made of rocks, ice, and dust. Saturn is the second largest planet and the second largest gas giant. Astronomers think Saturn has a small, rocky core deep inside, but most of the planet is made of gases.

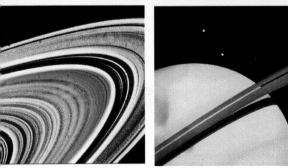

Saturn's rings twirl around the sixth planet in a wide, flat band.

Like Jupiter, Saturn spins very fast. One day on Saturn lasts only about eleven hours on Earth. Saturn orbits the Sun once every 29 and a half Earth years.

Many people think Saturn is the most beautiful planet of all.

CHAPTER 4

Far Out in Space

The gas giant Uranus looks like a big, blue-green ball. Uranus has many dark rings and at least twenty moons. One day on Uranus is about seventeen hours long. One year on this planet lasts eighty-four Earth years.

Although Neptune is the smallest gas giant, it is about four times bigger than Earth. Neptune travels around the Sun once every 165 Earth years. Like Earth, Neptune has winds. Neptune's winds are much stronger than Earth's winds. No one knows why, but hold on to your hat!

Wild winds form Neptune's Great Dark Spot, which is about the size of Earth.

GREAT DARK SPOT

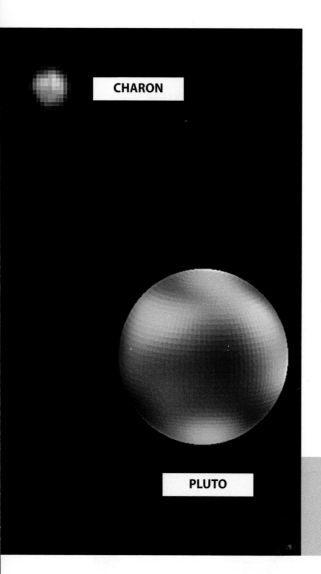

CHARON

PLUTO

No one saw Pluto until 1930. It is the smallest planet. It is also very far away. Frozen gases cover Pluto's rocky core. Pluto has a crooked orbit and takes nearly 248 Earth years to travel around the Sun.

This is a photograph of Pluto and its largest moon, Charon. They circle each other as they orbit the Sun.

Our Sun and its parade of planets lie along the edge of a galaxy known as the Milky Way. On a dark summer night, you can see the Milky Way. This bright, blurry path of stars is huge, but it is only a small part of a much larger universe. Someday, maybe you will help explore more of the universe.

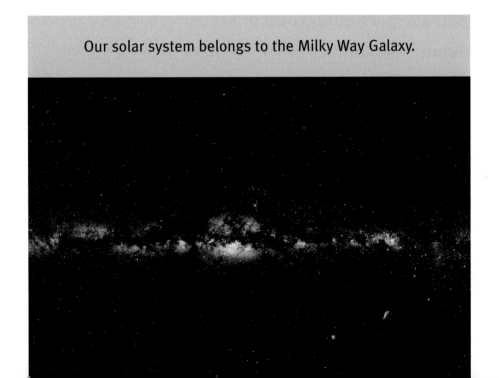

Our solar system belongs to the Milky Way Galaxy.

Glossary

astronomers — scientists who study stars, planets, and other parts of the universe

canyons — deep, narrow valleys with high, rocky sides

core — the center of an object

craters — round, bowl-shaped holes

galaxy — a giant group of stars

moon — an object in space that circles a larger object in space

planets — any of the large bodies in space that follow a set orbit around a star

solar — having to do with the Sun

universe — everything that exists, including Earth, the Sun, stars, and all objects, liquids, and gases

volcanoes — mountains that explode and send out hot gases, rocks, ashes, and lava (liquid rocks)

For More Information

Books

Extraordinary Solar System. Extraordinary Books (series). Stuart Atkinson (Scholastic)

The Planets. Space Explorer (series). Patricia Whitehouse (Heinemann Library)

The Solar System. Christine Corning Malloy (Chronicle Books)

Time For Kids: Planets! Editors of TIME for Kids (HarperCollins)

Web Sites

NASA Space Place
spaceplace.nasa.gov/en/kids/live/#
Visit NASA's Space Place for fascinating facts, games, and cartoons about space.

StarChild: A Learning Center for Young Astronomers
starchild.gsfc.nasa.gov/docs/StarChild/
solar_system_level1/planets.html
Learn about the planets and other bodies in our solar system.

Index

air 9, 10

canyons 12

craters 8

Earth 4, 5, 6, 8, 9, 10, 11, 14, 17, 18, 19

galaxies 21

gas giants 14, 16, 18, 19

Great Dark Spot, the 19

Great Red Spot, the 14

Milky Way 21

moons 7, 8, 12, 18, 20

planets 7, 8–13

rings 7, 15, 16

rocky 16

solar system 5, 12, 14

universe, the 21

volcanoes 9

water 9, 10

About the Author

Carol Ryback remembers saving her allowance to buy a school binder that featured the planets. She still finds outer space and other "scientific stuff" fascinating. A lifelong Wisconsin resident, Carol's favorite dog stars are golden retrievers Bailey, Merlin, and Harley Taylorson. When not stargazing, Carol likes to scuba dive.